Angels
WATCHING OVER ME

THIS BOOK BELONGS TO:

_____

The Manzo children

_____

from

Susie

with love & blessings

Angels
WATCHING OVER ME

p

This is a Parragon Publishing Book
This edition published in 2006

Parragon Publishing
Queen Street House
4 Queen Street
Bath BA1 1HE, UK

Project Director: Alice Wong
Designer: Timothy Shaner
Project Assistant: Lawrence Chesler
Editorial Research: Kathleen King, Nicholas Liu

Bible stories retold by Wendy Wax
Parables retold by Wendy Wax and Nicholas Liu
Activities by Monique Peterson and Alice Wong
Music arrangement by Frank Zuback

Printed in Singapore

10 9 8 7 6 5 4 3 2 1

Contents

Bible Stories

Bible Verses

Are we not
all children
of one Father?

MALACHI 2:10

The Creation

In the beginning, there was no world at all. No sun, no moon, no day, no night, no men, no women, no children. There was just God and darkness and the sounds of raging waters.

"Let there be light!" God said, and in no time (since there wasn't even time yet), warm, bright light appeared, chasing every bit of darkness away. God called the light "day" and the dark "night." Night would follow day, and day would follow night.

"It's good," God said, "but I'm not finished yet."

Night passed, day came. In the bright light all God could see was water—water above, water below, and water in between. Too much water and too little of anything else.

"Let there be a wide space where no waters flow!" God said, and suddenly a clear blue expanse broke through the waters, above and around. God called it "sky" and adorned it with white puffs called "clouds." The clouds held droplets of water so that God could cleanse all that lay below with a shower.

"It's good," God said, as the second day came to an end, "but I'm not finished yet."

The Creation

Night passed, day came. God gazed down at the giant waves below the clear, blue sky. "There's still too much water!" he said, watching the waves rock back and forth, back and forth.

"Let there be dry places among all this wetness!" God said, and then and there dark, dry patches began to poke up through the waters. God called these dry areas "land," and he called the waters, which now rolled onto sandy beaches, "seas." And that wasn't all . . . .

"Let plants and trees grow on the land!" God said. Instantly, the land looked as if a can of green paint had spilled over it. Green grass, green trees, green bushes . . . and soon other colorful vegetation appeared. There were cornstalks, grapevines, blueberry bushes, daisies, wild strawberries, and multicolored tulips carpeting the land.

"It's good," God said, as the third day came to an end, "but I'm not finished yet."

Night passed, day came. "Night is dark, day is light—but there is no in-between," God said, thoughtfully. And with no in-between, there was no way to tell what time of day or night it was.

"Let there be two great lights in

11

the sky to separate day from night!" God said, and that's when the sun and the moon came into being. The sun ruled day and the moon ruled night. Now there was a way to keep track of weeks, months, seasons, years, decades, and centuries.

"Since the sun is the brighter light," God said, "it shall come and go with grand style." He gathered every shade of red, blue, yellow, purple, and orange and whipped them into a dazzling sunrise and a brilliant sunset. God found them so beautiful, he continued making sunrise after sunrise, sunset after sunset, until he could be sure no two of them would

ever be alike. Then he made trillions of twinkling stars to shine around the moon so it wouldn't be lonesome.

"It's good," God said, as the fourth day came to an end, "but I'm not finished yet."

Night passed, day came. God looked down at the seas, then up at the sky. "So much space and so little in it!" God said. It was much too empty and silent.

"Let the seas and sky be filled with living creatures!" God said, and suddenly the silence broke into millions of sounds. Hummingbirds hummed, sparrows chirped, woodpeckers pecked, doves cooed, hawks screeched, geese honked, and billions of wings

The Creation

fluttered in the sky above, while fish splashed, dolphins sang, crabs crept, frogs croaked, and whales tooted in the seas below.

"It's good," God said, as the fifth day came to an end, "but I'm not finished yet."

Night passed, day came. God listened to a crow cawing in the sky above as he watched a minnow dart through shallow water. Suddenly, he noticed that the shallow water was filled with green leaves, vines, and roots. He looked up and noticed how quickly the plants, trees, and other vegetation were growing.

"Let the land be filled with living creatures," God said. "There is plenty for them to eat!" Instantly, the land was filled with roaring lions, buzzing bees, creeping lizards, scampering mice, growling bears, laughing hyenas, squealing pigs, wandering camels, slithering snakes, stomping elephants, waddling penguins, and many other animals. And that wasn't all. . . .

"Let there be someone just like me to care for the living creatures on land, in the sky, and in the seas!" God said, scooping up a handful of dust. He blew on it, and a man appeared before him—the first man in the world!

The Creation

The man squinted in the sunlight as he looked at God, and then at the world around him, with awe.

"I shall call you 'Adam,'" God said.

"Then Adam I am," the man said with a smile. He watched as God blew on another handful of dust to create a woman.

"What shall you call her?" Adam asked God.

"I'll leave that up to you," God said.

"I'll call you 'Eve,'" Adam said to the woman ("Eve" means "living").

"Then Eve I am," said the woman.

"You shall have lots of children," God said to them. "Teach them to take care of the world and the living creatures in it, for it is a very special place."

"We will," Adam and Eve promised.

"It's good," God said, as the sixth day came to an end. "And now I am finished. Tomorrow I shall rest!"

On the seventh day, while the sun shined high in the sky, and the daisies grew taller, and the horses galloped through the woods, and robins laid eggs in nests, and giraffes chomped on leafy treetops, and rabbits dug holes to live in, and fish swam in schools, and polar bears trod across ice, and monkeys swung from branch to branch, and Adam and Eve talked in the shade, God was peacefully asleep.

The Creation

by Cecil Francis Alexander

All things bright and beautiful,
    All creatures, great and small,
All things wise and wonderful,
    The Lord God made them all.

Each little flower that opens,
    Each little bird that sings,
He made their glowing colors,
    He made their tiny wings;

The rich man in his castle,
    The poor man at his gate,
God made them, high or lowly,
    And ordered their estate.

The purple-headed mountain,
    The river running by,
The sunset and the morning,
    That brightens up the sky;

16

The cold wind in the winter,
    The pleasant summer sun,
The ripe fruits in the garden—
    He made them every one.

The tall trees in the greenwood,
    The meadows where we play,
The rushes by the water
    We gather every day,—

He gave us eyes to see them,
    And lips that we might tell
How great is God Almighty,
    Who has made all things well!

And God saw every thing
that he had made, and,
behold, it was very good.

GENESIS 1:31

God's Creatures

How many are your

works, O Lord! In

wisdom you made

them all; the earth is

full of your creatures.

PSALM 104:24

Help your children feed and care for God's creatures. Maybe you'll make some new friends or witness the miracle of a caterpillar becoming a butterfly.

Bird Feeder

plastic gallon jug, scissors, wire hanger, birdseed

1. Cut a 5-inch circle out of the side of the jug, 2 inches from the bottom.
2. Untwist hanger and poke wire through the top of jug. Twist ends together.
3. Fill with birdseed to edge of hole. Hang on tree.

Corn Stake Feeder

piece of wood (12 x 4 inches), galvanized nails, corn

1. Drive a row of nails through the board, about 3 inches apart. Slide an ear of corn on each nail.
2. Put the feeder outdoors for squirrels, chipmunks, or rabbits.

Incubate a Butterfly

glass jar, caterpillar, leaves, wax paper, rubber band

1. Go on a caterpillar hunt during the spring and early summer. Look for one about the size of your little finger on trees. Carefully transfer it to your jar.
2. Cut a few small branches from the tree you found the caterpillar on and set aside in some water.
3. Cut a twig with several leaves from your branches and add to jar.
4. Cover the jar opening with wax paper. Seal it with a rubber band and poke several holes.
5. Give the caterpillar fresh leaves regularly.
6. The caterpillar will form a chrysalis and hatch in a few weeks. Gently ease it into the open air and watch your butterfly spread its wings.

Adam and Eve

od had created a beautiful world with one especially pretty place called Eden. Eden had sweeter-smelling flowers, greener plants, shadier trees, tastier fruits, and friendlier animals than any other place on earth. God chose this wonderful garden to be Adam and Eve's home, for he wanted them to be comfortable and happy.

"You may do as you like in Eden," God said, "as long as you follow one rule."

"Anything you say," Adam said to God.

God gestured toward two trees in the middle of the garden. "This is the Tree of Life," he said, pointing to one of them. "Anyone who eats its fruit will live forever and ever." Then he pointed to the other tree. "This is the Tree of Knowledge. Anyone who eats its fruit will know good and evil."

"What is the rule you'd like us to obey?" Eve asked.

"You must never, never, never eat fruit from the Tree of Knowledge," God said. "Don't even touch it or you will die."

Adam and Eve promised God they would never eat fruit from the Tree of Knowledge. It seemed like an easy rule to follow, especially as there was plenty of other fruit around.

So Adam and Eve settled into their new home. They spent the days strolling through the garden, wading in shallow brooks, making friends with animals, listening to birdcalls, gathering food, and picnicking under

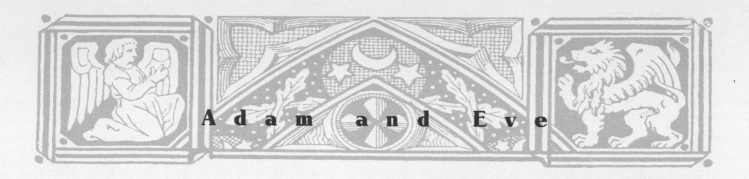

shady trees. At night, they lay under the stars, falling asleep to a chorus of chirping crickets. They were always naked, the way God created them, and never had a reason to be ashamed or afraid. They were good and they knew God loved them.

One day, Eve was gathering nuts near the Tree of Knowledge when a serpent crossed her path. What Eve didn't know was that the serpent was sneakier than the other animals.

"Is it true that God told you not to eat from the Tree of Knowledge?" the serpent asked.

"Yes," said Eve. "He said we would die if we touched it."

"And you believed him?" hissed the serpent.

Eve nodded innocently.

Adam and Eve

"God is just trying to protect you from knowing the difference between good and evil," the serpent hissed. "But don't you think you have a right to know the difference? God does, so why shouldn't you?"

Eve turned to the Tree of Knowledge and, for the first time, looked closely at its ripe, red fruit. She wondered whether it was sweet or sour.

"Don't you want to know all that God knows?" the serpent teased.

"Well...I am curious," Eve said, her mouth starting to water. And before she could stop herself, she plucked the fruit from the branch and took a small bite. It tasted stranger than the other fruits in the garden. "I'll give

Adam a taste," she said, turning back toward the serpent—but it had disappeared.

Eve found Adam playing with a family of monkeys. "Here, Adam," she said, holding out the fruit. "Taste this. It's from the Tree of Knowledge."

"But we promised God..." Adam began.

"I know," Eve said, "but aren't you just a bit curious?"

Adam bit into the fruit.

Suddenly, a cold wind swept over them though the sun still shone brightly in the sky. Shivering, they tried to cover up their nakedness with fig leaves. For the first time in their lives they were afraid, and they

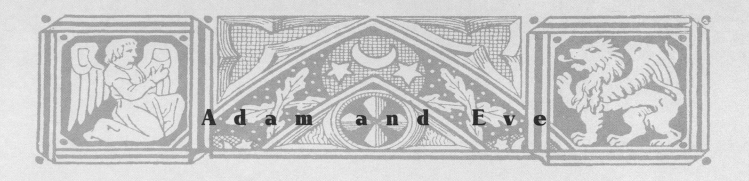

could hear God approaching!

"Let's hide!" Adam said, pulling Eve behind a tree. But it was no use hiding from God. When he saw them covering up their naked bodies and shivering in the cold, he knew they had disobeyed him.

"Have you eaten the fruit from the Tree of Knowledge?" God asked Adam.

"Y-yes," Adam said, bowing his head. "Eve gave it to me."

"Is that true?" God said, looking at Eve.

"Yes," Eve said, bowing her head. "The serpent tricked me."

Though God still loved Adam and Eve, he had to punish them. "I must now forbid you from eating fruit from the Tree of Life," he said sadly. "You shall not live forever and ever as I will."

"We'll obey you this time!" Adam and Eve said to God.

"That's what you said the last time," God said, "and you went back on your word. Just to be sure you don't disobey me this time, you must leave Eden—permanently."

So clinging to each other with their heads bowed, Adam and Eve went into the large, unfamiliar world. Would they find enough food? How would they protect themselves from dangerous animals? Would they know a poisonous plant if they saw one? The only things they were sure of were that God still loved them and that there was no turning back.

✳

Prayers

God bless all those that I love;
God bless all those that love me:
God bless all those that love those that I love
And all those that love those that love me.

Amen.

Dear Father, hear and bless
Thy beasts and singing birds,
And guard with tenderness
Small things that have no words.

Amen.

Hurt No Living Thing

by Christina Rossetti

Hurt no living thing;
    Ladybird, nor butterfly,
    Nor moth with dusty wing,
Nor cricket chirping cheerily,
Nor grasshopper so light of leap,
    Nor dancing gnat, nor beetle fat,
    Nor harmless worms that creep.

Noah's Ark

any, many years passed after Adam and Eve had left Eden. They had had lots of children, and now had grandchildren, great grandchildren, and great great grandchildren! God hoped the offspring of Adam and Eve would respect the earth and care for the animals, but it turned out they did no such thing. Instead, these people became mean and selfish, and often acted in horrible ways. They had stopped listening to God.

"I'm sorry I ever created these people," God said, sadly. "I shall destroy the world and start over." But first he went to see a man named Noah.

Noah was six hundred years old and had three sons, Shem, Ham, and Jepheth. Noah was kind and honest, and he always obeyed God.

"Noah," God said, when he found him. "I plan to cause a huge flood to wash over the earth. Everyone will drown—except for you and your family and some animals."

Noah listened carefully as God told him what to do.

"Build an ark of wood with large rooms inside, and be sure to seal all the cracks with pitch to keep the water out," God instructed. Then he gave him the exact measurements of the wood. "It will have three decks, a window near the top, and a door on the side.

"When the seas begin to rise, this ark will be a safe place for you and your wife, your three sons and their wives."

Noah's Ark

"I'll do as you say," Noah said, grateful that he and his family were to be spared.

"But why do we need such a large ark?"

"Because you are to bring with you two of each living creature, one male and one female, so that they can multiply in the new world. And you'll need lots of food, too."

Noah rounded up his sons and they got right to work. They measured and hammered, sawed and sanded, and soon the ark began to take shape.

"What a stupid thing to make," a neighbor said to Noah.

"What do you expect from such a crazy old man?" said another neighbor.

But Noah didn't listen to any of them. He listened only to God.

When the ark was finally finished, Noah and his sons rounded up the animals. Then, at last, they were ready to board the ark.

First, Noah led his family up the wooden plank that led to the highest deck. Next came the animals, two by two. Grrrrrr. Grrrrr. Cluck. Cluck. Stomp. Stomp. Quack. Quack. Ruff. Ruff. Neigh. Neigh. Tweet. Tweet. Squeak! Squeak! Mooo! Mooo!

Noah's Ark

Wh-ish. Wh-ish. Cheep. Cheep. Snort. Snort. Oink. Oink. Hiss! Hiss! Meow! Meow! Hyenas, goats, peacocks, zebras, turtles, camels, giraffes, doves, hippopotami, pheasants, bears, penguins, donkeys, lizards, rabbits, frogs, buffalo, sheep, and every other animal imaginable climbed aboard with its mate. Some had spots, some were striped, some were huge, some were tiny, some were loud, some were quiet…what a magnificent parade!

"They'll never be able to drag that boat to the sea," a neighbor said, having no idea about the floods. "It's much too heavy." The other neighbors laughed.

Just as Noah and his sons pulled up the wooden plank the sky grew cloudy. Then it began to sprinkle.

By the time they showed the pigs to their sty near the middle deck, the horses to their stables near the upper deck, the chickens to their coops near the front of the ark, the kittens to their basket near the back of the ark, and the other animals to their own special areas, the rain started coming down.

Pitter-patter, pitter-patter. The drops splattered against the shutters of the window near the top of the boat.

Pitter-patter, pitter-patter. The drops splattered against the window shutters of a nearby house where people were pushing and shoving for

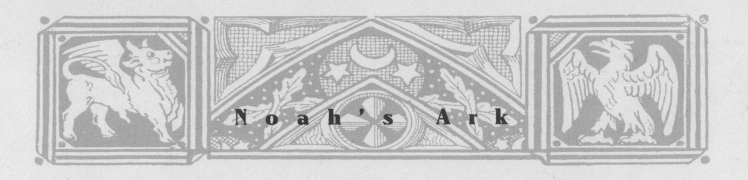

a place to look out. They all wanted to watch the ark as puddles formed around it.

B-O-OOM! Thunder crashed. Lightning flashed. The rain pounded and poured as the wind picked up strength and speed. On land, roofs began to leak, puddles poured into other puddles, and people grew frantic. Noah's ark no longer seemed like such a bad idea to them. For forty days and forty nights, it rained and poured. Puddles became rivers and rivers became seas. The ark tossed and turned as giant waves crashed thousands of feet in the air! The last of the rooftops and treetops and mountaintops had long since disappeared beneath the floods. But Noah, his family, and the animals were safe and dry inside the ark.

At the end of the fortieth day, the rain suddenly stopped. Everything was silent and still, and the ark rocked gently in the water. Noah hurried to the window and gasped. All he saw was water—water everywhere. Not a house or tree or mountain in sight! "God has done what he set out to do," he announced to the others. "The old world is gone forever!"

Then he beckoned to a raven.

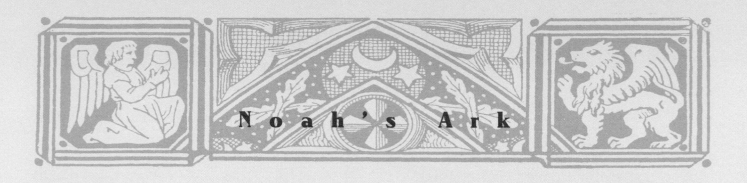

Noah's Ark

The raven left its mate and flew over to Noah.

"Fly out to look for dry land," Noah said to the raven. "When you find it, come back and show us the way."

After the raven flew out the window, Noah flung open the door and led his wife, and then his sons and their wives, onto the upper deck of the ark. Next came two panthers, then two pandas, then two crocodiles, two blue jays, and two swans. Soon all three decks were completely full!

It had been so long since they had been outside, and the fresh air felt wonderful! Two days later the raven returned. It looked tired and hungry—and it hadn't found an inch of land. It hadn't even found a place to perch!

Next, Noah sent out a dove. The dove was gone for many months and finally returned with an olive leaf in its beak.

"The water must be going down!" Noah said. "The land is finally drying up!"

After a hearty meal and a good night's cuddle with its mate, the dove flew out again. While it was gone, the waters got lower and lower until small islands, and then larger pieces of land, began to poke through. This time, the dove didn't return—but no one seemed to mind.

Noah's Ark

"It's time to leave the ark," God said to Noah one day. "Bring your wife, and your sons and their wives, and bring every pair of animals so they can have lots of babies. Welcome to the new world!"

When they drifted onto land, Noah and his sons set up the wooden plank and two by two the animals left the ark. The tigers prowled down the plank. The chickens scrambled down the plank. The elephants climbed down the plank. The ducks waddled down the plank. The puppies scurried down the plank. The horses galloped down the plank. The canaries fluttered down the plank. The mice scampered down the plank. The cows roamed down the plank. The worms wiggled down the plank. The monkeys swung down the plank. The bulls charged down the plank. The pigs scuffled down the plank. The snakes slithered down the plank. The kittens pattered down the plank. And all the other animals followed behind them.

Next came Noah's sons and their wives.

And last, Noah and his wife came down the plank. It felt strange to walk on dry land, for they had been on the ark for so long!

Noah and his family sat on the ground and thanked God for taking care of them.

When God heard their thanks, he gave them a beautiful gift in the sky— a dazzling rainbow, the first ever.

Noah's Ark

You are to bring

into the ark two of

all living creatures,

male and female,

to keep them alive

with you.

Genesis 6:19

The next time it rains, imagine with your children what it must have been like for Noah and all the animals on the ark while it rained for forty days and nights! Then get busy and make an ark of your own, complete with animals. How many animals can you make before the rain stops?

Shoebox Ark

cardboard shoebox, markers, scissors, popsicle sticks, glue

1. Draw door and windows on the sides of the box and cut along their outlines. Leave a hinge of cardboard on the door so it can open and close. The door should also be about an inch from the bottom of the box.
2. Lay 3 or 4 popsicle sticks together to make a plank. Break 2 or 3 popsicle sticks in half and glue them across the plank to hold it in place.
3. Decorate the ark with markers. You can draw lines to indicate strips of wood or add rolling blue waves to the bottom of the ark.

Two by Two

flour, salt, water, food coloring, toothpicks, seeds, rice, sequins, notions

1. Mix one part flour, two parts salt, and two parts water in a bowl until the consistency is like clay.
2. Separate the dough into several balls. Add a different food coloring to each ball for a variety of colors.
3. Create animal bodies by rolling chunks of clay into little balls. Make smaller balls for heads. Use toothpicks to reinforce legs, giraffe necks, or elephant trunks. Add seeds for eyes, wild rice for porcupine quills, or sequins for leopard spots.
4. Let dry for a few days.

Amazing Grace

2. 'Twas grace that taught my heart to fear,
   And grace my fears relieved;
   How precious did that grace appear
   The hour I first believed!

3. Through many dangers, toils, and snares,
   I have already come;
   'Tis grace hath brought me safe thus far,
   And grace will lead me home.

4. The Lord has promised good to me,
   His word my hope secures;
   He will my shield and portion be
   As long as life endures.

5. And when this flesh and heart shall fail,
   And mortal life shall cease;
   I shall possess within the veil
   A life of joy and peace.

Prayers

Please give me what I ask, dear Lord,
If you'd be glad about it,
But if you think it's not for me,
Please help me do without it.

Amen.

Lord, teach me all that I should know;
In grace and wisdom I may grow;
The more I learn to do Thy will,
The better may I love Thee still.

Isaac Watts

The Story of Joseph

any years ago, in a place called Hebron, a shepherd named Jacob had twelve sons. His favorite was his eleventh son, Joseph. For this reason, Joseph's older brothers were jealous of him—especially when their father made him a beautiful coat. The coat was embroidered with intricate patterns of purple, red, blue, and yellow, and Joseph wore it everywhere.

One night, Joseph had a strange dream that seemed real. The next morning, he put on his special coat and raced out to the pasture to tell his brothers about it. (Joseph liked his brothers even though they were mean to him.)

"Those bright colors might scare away the flock," said Reuben, the oldest brother, when he saw Joseph still a mile away.

"He's too in love with himself to care," said Judah.

"Brothers!" Joseph said breathlessly, as he approached. "Last night I dreamt we were all out in the pasture tying grain into bundles. My bundle leapt out of my arms and stood straight up in front of me. Then all your bundles leapt out of your hands, formed a circle around my bundle, and bowed down to it."

"You're not a king!" Judah said angrily.

"We'd never bow down to you!" said Simon.

But Joseph ignored his brothers' nastiness—he was used to it.

A few days later, Joseph had

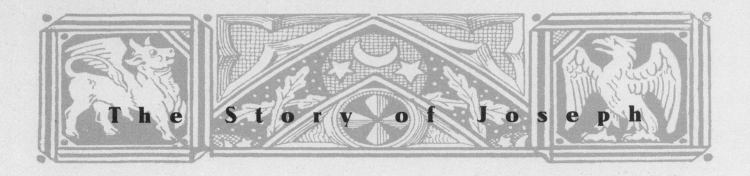

another dream. Again he put on his coat of many colors and went to tell his brothers.

"Last night I dreamt that the sun and the moon and eleven stars were bowing down to me," he said, smiling.

"We have better things to do than listen to your silly dreams," his brothers yelled angrily.

But when Joseph told his father about the dream, Jacob didn't think it was silly at all. Could I be the sun, my wife Rachel the moon, and my eleven other sons the stars that bow down to Joseph in the dream, he wondered?

One day, Jacob sent his oldest sons and their flocks to a far-off pasture where he had heard grass and water were plentiful. A few days later, he sent Joseph to check on them.

Joseph climbed hill after hill, and crossed valley after valley, until he finally saw his brothers and their flocks in the distance.

"There's that colorful coat again," Judah said to his brothers.

"Let's kill him so we won't have to listen to his silly dreams," said Levi.

"I have a better idea," said Reuben. "Let's dig a hole, throw him in, and leave him to die alone." The others liked this idea even better, not knowing that Reuben secretly planned to rescue Joseph when they weren't looking. Being the oldest brother he felt responsible—and he knew it was wrong to kill.

They quickly dug a deep hole and waited. When Joseph approached,

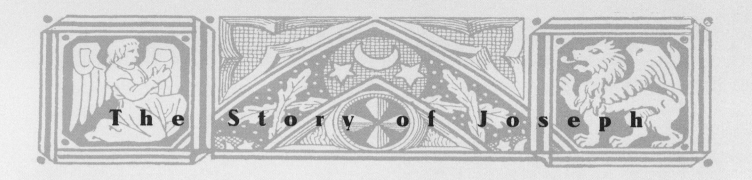
they grabbed him, tore off his color-ful coat, and threw him into the hole.

"LET ME OUT OF HERE!" Joseph cried. "HE-E-ELP!"

Later in the day, a caravan of merchants came by on their way to Egypt to sell spices.

"Let's sell Joseph to the merchants," Judah said to his brothers. "After all, he is our brother and leaving him in the hole to die is a bit harsh." The others agreed and quickly fetched Joseph from the hole. They sold him for twenty shekels of silver.

"What shall we tell our father?" Judah said guiltily. "He'll want to know where his favorite son is."

After much thought they decid-ed to slaughter a goat and dip Joseph's coat in its blood. And that's just what they did.

"Look what we found!" Reuben said to their father when they returned to Hebron. "Isn't this the coat you made for Joseph?"

As Jacob examined the coat his eyes filled with tears. "Yes, indeed, this is my eleventh son's coat," he

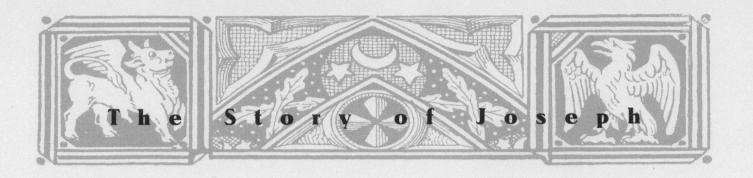

said sadly. "A ferocious animal must have eaten him." He then spent many days mourning for Joseph.

Meanwhile, Joseph arrived in Egypt and was sold as a slave to a rich man named Potiphar. As soon as Joseph met Potiphar, he knew God was taking care of him, for Potiphar was very kind. Instead of making Joseph build pyramids in the hot sun, Potiphar gave him an easy job in the palace. "Make sure the maids keep the house clean and the cook prepares good meals," he said. And that's just what Joseph did for many years—always making sure to do a good job so that God would be happy.

One day, while Potiphar was out of town, Potiphar's wife noticed how handsome Joseph had become. "Come to my bedroom," she said to him.

Now, most men would have gone, for Potiphar's wife was very beautiful, but Joseph just shook his head. "You're very pretty," he said, "but it would not be right."

Feeling hurt and rejected, she ripped Joseph's cloak and took it from him. When Potiphar returned, his wife showed him the torn cloak and told him that Joseph had attacked her—of course, this was a lie. Potiphar believed his wife and had Joseph thrown into prison.

As a prisoner, Joseph kept his cell clean, shared his food with the other prisoners, and prayed to God to set him free. When the other prisoners had strange dreams, they relied on Joseph to tell them what they meant.

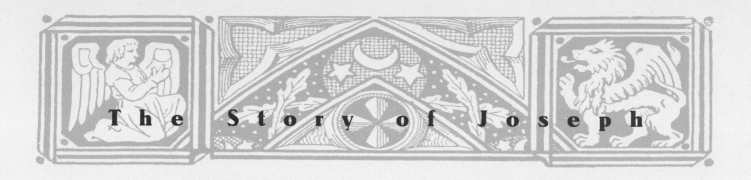
"Thank you, Joseph," they would say. "Don't thank me, thank God," he would answer them.

One time, Joseph told a prisoner that his dream meant he'd be rescued in three days. When the dream came true, Joseph said, "Please mention me to the Pharaoh." (You see, the prisoner was the Pharaoh's cup bearer— the one responsible for keeping his wine cup full.)

One night, after Joseph had been in prison for two years, the Pharaoh had a confusing dream. In the morning, he called for his wise men and told them his dream. "Tell me what it means," he said to them.

But though they checked their charts and scrolls, the wise men couldn't help him.

"I know someone who can tell you what your dream means," the Pharaoh's cup bearer said, for he remembered his promise to Joseph over two years before. "His name is Joseph, and he's in prison."

"Then free him!" the Pharaoh ordered. "And bring him to me at once!"

"Can you tell me what my dream means?" the Pharaoh asked Joseph, when he stood before him in fresh, clean clothes.

"I can't," said Joseph, "but God can. What did you dream?"

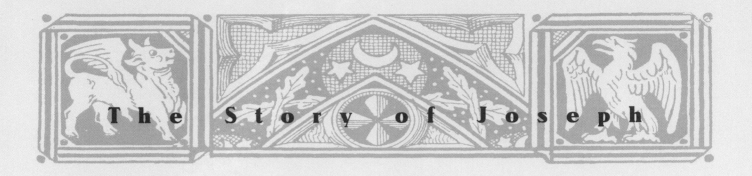

"In my dream, seven fat cows came out of the River Nile. Then seven thin cows came out of the river and ate the fat cows. But when they finished eating, they were just as thin as before. Then I had another dream. Seven pieces of healthy grain were growing on a single stalk. Soon, seven withered pieces of grain sprouted and swallowed the healthy grain. What does it mean?"

"Please, God," Joseph prayed silently. "What does it mean?" And suddenly he knew, for God had a way of opening Joseph's mind.

"Pharaoh," Joseph said, "both dreams mean the same thing. There will be plenty to eat and drink during the next seven years. But during the seven years after that, the crops won't grow and everyone will go hungry— unless something is done about it."

"Your God really is with you!" the Pharaoh said, truly amazed. "I trust you more than I trust anyone else. From now on, you will rule my palace and make sure that plenty of food is put in storage so that no one will starve when the crops stop growing. You will be the greatest man in Egypt, except for myself, of course."

Joseph couldn't believe his ears! Only a few hours earlier he had been a prisoner and now he was asked to rule over Egypt alongside the Pharaoh! Joseph knew he had only God to thank for this.

Sure enough, the Pharaoh's dream did come true. And when hard times came, Joseph handed out

the food that he'd been storing for seven years. When people in other lands heard that there was food in Egypt, they went there hoping to have some for themselves. Joseph's brothers were among these hungry people.

When Joseph's brothers arrived in Egypt, they bowed before the governor of the land—whom they didn't recognize as their brother Joseph! (He was older and more handsome than they remembered.) Joseph, however, knew his brothers right away and told them who he was. At first his brothers were afraid of him. They remembered his dream from long ago and understood that it had come true—they now really were bowing down to him.

"Brothers, there's nothing to be afraid of!" Joseph said warmly. "I don't blame you for anything. God meant for me to be here!" Then he and his brothers hugged and kissed with forgiveness. Joseph, their brother, had the heart of a king.

Joseph's brothers went home and told their father that his son was alive. Soon after that, the whole family moved to Egypt to be near Joseph.

He's Got the Whole World

He's got the whole world __ in His hands, __ He's got the
whole world __ in his Hands, __ He's got the
whole world ___ in His hands, ___ He's got the
whole world in His hands.

2. He's got the little, bitty baby in His hands. . .

3. He's got you and me brother . . .

4. He's got you and me sister . . .

5. He's got everybody here. . .

6. He's got the wind and the rain. . .

7. He's got the sun and the moon . . .

8. He's got the whole world . . .

Baby Moses

oseph's family lived in Egypt for many years and multiplied there. As the generations grew larger and larger, they became known as the Israelites, or people of Israel.

Four hundred years after Joseph's family arrived, a cruel Pharaoh came to rule the land. "There are too many Israelites in Egypt," he warned. "If we don't do something soon, they'll become more powerful than us."

The Egyptians listened as Pharaoh gave them orders.

"Make the people of Israel your slaves!" he commanded. "Have them work till they're too tired to have more children."

The Egyptians obeyed their king—they had no choice! They forced the Israelites to be their slaves and demanded that they make bricks and build with them until their shoulders were sore, their backs ached, and their feet were blistered. But still the people of Israel kept having children.

This made Pharaoh even angrier! "From now on," he commanded, "if an Israelite woman gives birth to a baby boy, he must be killed!"

One day, an Israelite woman gave birth to a beautiful baby boy. For three months, the baby stayed hidden inside while the woman, her husband, their daughter, and their son (who'd been born before the rule) tried to come up with a way to save their youngest family member. They prayed to God to send them an idea.

Baby Moses

"I've got it!" the mother said one morning. Her husband and children watched as she wove a basket out of reeds. She then wrapped the tiny baby in soft blankets and placed him in the basket. "Come, Miriam," she said to her daughter. And the two of them walked down to the riverbank.

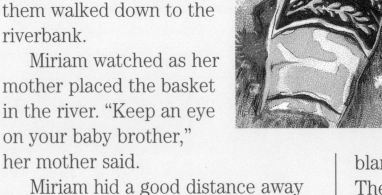

Miriam watched as her mother placed the basket in the river. "Keep an eye on your baby brother," her mother said.

Miriam hid a good distance away from the riverbank and watched the basket.

"What's that?" said a voice.

Miriam looked up and saw Pharaoh's daughter, a princess, and her servants approaching the riverbank to bathe in the river. The princess had spotted the basket. Miriam watched as one of the servants plucked the basket out of the water and brought it to the princess.

"What a beautiful baby!" she cried, peering into the basket. The baby had kicked off his blankets and was crying with hunger. The princess scooped him out of the basket and rocked him gently. "He has such wise eyes," she said. "He must belong to an Israelite woman."

The princess knew about her father's order to kill all Israelite baby boys. But how could such a precious baby be killed? "I'll keep him for myself," she said. "I must find a nurse who can feed him."

At that moment, Miriam came out of hiding. "Would you like me to get an Israelite woman to care for the baby?" Miriam asked.

"I would like that very much," the princess said, smiling. "Fetch her at once—this baby is very hungry."

Miriam raced home and quickly brought her mother back to the riverbank.

"Can you take care of this baby for me?" the princess asked Miriam's mother. "I will pay you."

"I-I'd love to!" the baby's mother said, trying desperately to hold back tears of joy.

"You can bring him back to me when he's old enough to eat on his own," said the princess. "Then I shall adopt him and see that he has a good education and the life of a prince."

So the baby went back to his family to be nursed and cared for by his real mother. His mother thanked God over and over for listening to her prayers. When the baby was three years old, she brought him to the princess who named him Moses ("Moses" means "drawn out," which was fitting since the princess had drawn him out of the river). One day, Moses would become a very important leader in Egypt.

Kum Ba Yah
(Come By Here)

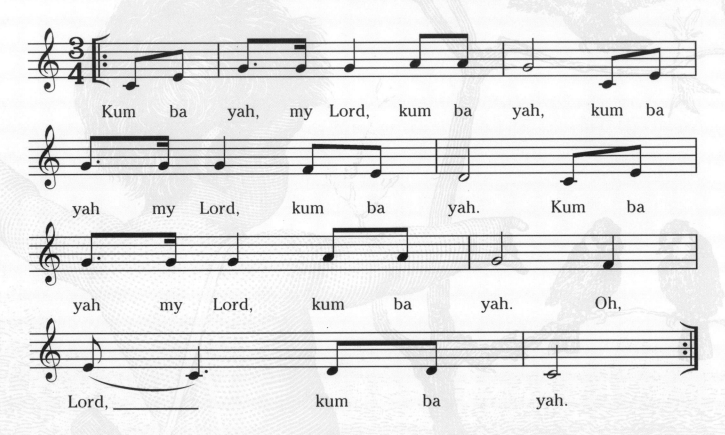

Kum ba yah, my Lord, kum ba yah, kum ba

yah my Lord, kum ba yah. Kum ba

yah my Lord, kum ba yah. Oh,

Lord, _____ kum ba yah.

2. Someone's crying, Lord, Kum ba yah,

3. Someone's laughing, Lord . . .

4. Someone's singing, Lord . . .

5. Someone's praying, Lord . . .

6. Kum ba yah my Lord . . .

*This is the day which
the Lord has made;
let us rejoice and
be glad in it.*

PSALM 118:24

Let Us Make a Joyful Noise

Let them praise

his name with

dancing and make

music to him

with tambourine

and harp.

PSALM 149:3

Children love making music. Form a band! Create instruments together and decorate with construction paper and markers. Then, sing songs of praise.

Shakers

dried beans or rice, small tin cans, masking tape

1. Fill cans about half full with dried beans or rice.
2. Cover with plastic lid, if available, or tape.
3. Experiment for different sounds and rhythms. Hold the shaker sideways and tip it slowly so the beans slide from one end to the other. Or shake it quickly up and down for a loud rattle.

Tambourines

2 heavy-duty paper plates, a handful of dried corn or peas, masking tape

1. Place the dried corn or peas on one plate. Cover it with the other plate.
2. Tape the edges together to form a tight seal.
3. Hold your tambourine with one hand and tap it with the other. How many ways can you vary the sound? Use your palm or fingertips or try slapping it against your leg.

Box Harp

shoebox with lid, large rubber bands, pencil, 3 x $\frac{1}{2}$-inch rubber eraser

1. Stretch the rubber bands around the box.
2. Slide the pencil under the rubber bands to create a bridge. Wedge the eraser underneath one end of the pencil. Pluck.

Variation: To make a Box Zither, cut a hole in the lid of the shoebox before stretching the rubber bands across. Slide a pencil under the rubber bands on either side of the hole.

We Thank Thee

by Ralph Waldo Emerson

For flowers that bloom about our feet;
For tender grass so fresh and sweet;
For song of bird and hum of bee;
For all things fair we hear or see—
    Father in Heaven, we thank Thee!

For blue of stream, and blue of sky;
For pleasant shade of branches high;
For fragrant air and cooling breeze;
For beauty of the blooming trees—
    Father in Heaven, we thank Thee!

Prayers

For mother-love, for father-care;
For brothers strong and sisters fair;
For love at home and school each day;
For guidance lest we go astray—
    Father in Heaven, we thank Thee!

For Thy dear, everlasting arms,
That bear us o'er all ills and harms;
For blessed words of long ago,
That help us now Thy will to know—
    Father in Heaven, we thank Thee!

Jesus Loves Me

Je - sus loves me, this I know, for the Bi - ble tells me so;

Lit - tle ones to Him be - long, They are weak, but He is strong.

Yes, Je - sus loves me, Yes, Je - sus loves me,

Yes, Je - sus loves me, The Bi - ble tells me so.

Growing Plants & Flowers

. . . whoever sows

generously will also

reap generously.

2 Corinthians 9:6

Jesus said even faith as small as a mustard seed can move mountains. Show your children what a little seed or bulb can become. Plant mustard! Radishes also sprout quickly and are easy to grow. Or bring nature inside with a bit of indoor gardening.

Seeds of Faith
egg carton, soil, mustard seeds

1. Fill each egg compartment with soil.
2. Poke a ¼-inch hole in each pocket of soil. Drop in 2 or 3 seeds and cover.
3. Water, keeping the soil evenly moist. Seeds will sprout within a week.

Sow a Garden
radish seeds, garden plot

1. In early spring, turn over a row of dirt.
2. With a stick, dig a trench about ¼-inch deep.
3. Sprinkle seeds into trench and cover with dirt.
4. When sprouts are 2 inches high (about 1½ weeks), thin out seedlings. Give sprouts at least an inch of growing room on either side.
5. Radishes will be ready to eat in three to four weeks.

Force Bulbs
large glass saucer or pie plate, gravel, bulbs (tulip, daffodil, or narcissus)

1. Place bulbs in saucer and cover them with gravel. Be sure to leave the bulb tips slightly exposed.
2. Fill the bottom of the saucer with water.
3. Store in a cool, dark closet or cupboard.
4. Maintain water level and watch as roots and shoots grow.
5. In about six weeks, bring your bulbs into the daylight and watch them bloom.

David and Goliath

There was once a very greedy king named Saul. God was so disappointed with King Saul's selfish ways that he chose a young shepherd named David to replace him when the time came. David, the youngest of eight brothers, had a warm smile and a generous heart.

While David tended sheep in the pasture, God often spoke to him. Whether he was chasing away wolves with his slingshot, playing his harp and singing, or having lunch under a tree, David always stopped what he was doing to listen. And as David grew older, he felt himself growing closer and closer to God.

At the time, many battles were being fought between the Israelites and the Philistines. David always knew about them because three of his brothers were King Saul's soldiers. His father, Jesse, often asked David to bring his brothers bread and cheese. That way, he could find out how his sons were doing.

One day, when David brought food to his brothers in their camp in the Valley of Elah, he found them huddled together with the other Israelite soldiers. They were talking about a new Philistine soldier from Gath named Goliath.

"I'm not fighting with Goliath on the other side!" said the bravest soldier.

"Me neither," said the strongest soldier. "He's not going to stick me with that three-hundred-pound

bronze sword or that five-hundred-pound iron spear."

"Did you see the size of him?" exclaimed David's tallest brother. "I wouldn't get in his way for all the silver in the world!"

"King Saul says we must fight," said David's smartest brother. "But what good would that do us? We have no chance of winning."

David couldn't believe his ears! He had never heard his brothers or the other Israelite soldiers talk this way. Usually they were brave, strong, and confident.

THUMP, THUMP, THUMP, THUMP. Heavy footsteps rumbled and shook the ground as they approached the Israelite camp. When David saw who it was he couldn't believe his eyes. There in front of them was the biggest, strongest, ugliest, meanest man he had ever seen. Not a man—a giant!

"CHOOSE A MAN TO FIGHT ME!" Goliath said in a loud, booming voice. "IF HE WINS THE FIGHT AND KILLS ME, WE WILL BECOME YOUR SLAVES. BUT IF I WIN THE FIGHT AND KILL HIM, YOU WILL BECOME OUR SLAVES."

Though it was difficult to do, David tore his eyes away from the giant to see how the Israelite soldiers would respond. They were all trembling with fear, including King Saul, who had just arrived. When he saw the giant, he dove

David and Goliath

behind the nearest bush.

"You heard the giant!" King Saul yelled from behind the bush. "One of you cowards has to fight him. Line up, and choose who that will be."

"But . . ." said the few soldiers who were brave enough to speak.

"But nothing," King Saul shouted. "Go to it!"

David watched the Israelite soldiers line up on one side of the battlefield while the Philistine soldiers lined up on the other side. None of them went to Goliath who stood in the center.

"WHO'S IT GOING TO BE?" Goliath boomed, glaring at each of the Israelite soldiers, one by one.

"One of my soldiers had bet-ter speak up soon," King Saul hissed from his hiding place. He didn't notice the young shepherd boy who stood nearby.

"I'll fight Goliath," David whispered to King Saul.

King Saul peered out from behind the bush, noticing David for the first time. "What's that, boy?" he asked.

"I said 'I'll fight Goliath,'" David repeated confidently. He knew God would watch over him, and he didn't feel afraid at all.

"Run along home, boy," King Saul said. "This is no time for jokes. You're much too young and skinny and. . . ."

While the King babbled on and on, David picked up his staff, chose five smooth stones

73

David and Goliath

from a nearby stream, and put them into his bag. Then he walked boldly out to the battlefield. He didn't stop until he was face to face—actually, face to ankle—with Goliath.

"I'll fight you!" David shouted up at the giant. He had to yell it a few times before Goliath even heard him.

"IS THAT A MOUSE I HEAR?" Goliath asked, peering down at the ground. When he saw David, he began to laugh. "HA HA HA HA HA!" he roared. "DO YOU REALLY THINK YOU CAN KILL ME WITH THAT WIMPY SLINGSHOT?"

In the loudest voice he could muster, David said, "You come against me with a three-hundred-pound bronze sword and a five-hundred-pound iron spear. But I come against you in the name of God—the God of the people of Israel." Then quickly, he reached into his bag, pulled out a stone, and loaded his slingshot. David aimed and. . . .

SMACK! The stone hit Goliath right in the middle of his forehead. Goliath fell to the ground, face first, with a loud crash. David had won!

No one could believe their eyes—David's brothers, the other soldiers, and King Saul were completely stunned. When they got over their shock, they began to shout: "We're free! The Philistines are now are slaves! Young David won our battle!"

And so the Israelites celebrated. Little did they know then that the young, brave boy who slayed the giant would one day be their king. ✳

The Lord is my shepherd; I shall not want.

He maketh me to lie down in green pastures:
he leadeth me beside the still waters.

He restoreth my soul: he leadeth me in
the paths of righteousness for his name's sake.

Yea, though I walk through the valley
of the shadow of death, I will fear no evil:
for thou art with me; thy rod and thy
staff they comfort me.

Thou preparest a table before me
in the presence of mine enemies:
thou anointest my head with oil;
my cup runneth over.

Surely goodness and mercy shall
follow me all the days of my
life: and I will dwell in the
house of the Lord for ever.

PSALM 23

Let There Be Light

God saw that the

light was good, and

he separated the light

from the darkness.

GENESIS 1:4

Start the week by celebrating the first day of creation. Make a mobile frame out of a tree branch with many twigs and string on heavenly bodies you make. Imagine with your children that the finished mobile is the hand of God, holding the sun, moon, and stars.

Shining Sun

red, orange & yellow tissue paper, scissors, glue, clear plastic round lid, hole punch, string

1. Draw triangular sunrays half the length of the lid on tissue paper. Cut out.
2. Spread a thin layer of glue on the lid. Paste on tissue rays to create a circle of colored rays.
4. Shine light through lid to see different colors.
5. Punch a hole near edge. Tie string through hole and tie to branch.

Foil Moon

cardboard, marker, scissors, aluminum foil, hole punch, string

1. Draw crescent and full moons on cardboard. Cut out.
2. Wrap each completely with aluminum foil.
3. Punch a hole near edge. Tie string through hole and tie to branch.

Glittering Stars

cardboard, marker, scissors, glue, glitter (gold, silver, blue), hole punch, string

1. Draw different-sized stars on cardboard. Vary them by making longer or shorter points.
2. Spread a thin layer of glue on top.
3. Sprinkle each with a different color glitter. Let dry. Repeat on other side.
4. Punch a hole near edge. Tie string through hole and tie to branch.

Shining Light

L et your light shine! Help your children make personalized candleholders. Light a candle during evening prayers. At Christmastime, go caroling with windproof tin lanterns.

Stained Glass Lantern

glue, glass pint jars, colored tissue paper, scissors, paintbrush, candle

1. Squeeze 2 tablespoons of glue into a jar. Thin with water until the consistency is like milk.
2. Cut different shapes, sizes, and colors of tissue paper.
3. Brush the outside of a second jar with glue solution.
4. Overlap the tissue paper shapes on the glass and brush over them with glue solution. Let dry.
5. Place a candle in the bottom of the glass. Light and watch the room fill with color.

Tin Can Lantern

large tin can, marker, large nail, hammer, wire coat hanger, candle

1. Fill the can with water and place in a freezer until frozen.
2. With a marker, draw stars, moon, or sun patterns on the outside of the can.
3. Carefully poke holes along your markings with a hammer and nail.
4. For the handle, poke two holes near the top of the can directly opposite one another.
5. Melt and remove the ice.
6. Bend the hanger and loop the ends through the handle holes. Twist ends to secure.
7. Place a candle in your lantern.

Let your light shine before men, that they may see your good deeds and praise your Father in heaven.

MATTHEW 5:16

79

This Little Light of Mine

This lit-tle light of mine, I'm gon-na let it shine.

This lit-tle light of mine, I'm gon-na let it shine, let it

shine, let it shine, let it shine.

2. Hide it under a bushel? NO!
   I'm gonna let it shine.
   Hide it under a bushel? NO!
   I'm gonna let it shine, let it shine,
   let it shine, let it shine.

3. Don't let Satan blow it out,
   I'm gonna let it shine,
   Don't let Satan blow it out,
   I'm gonna let it shine, let it shine,
   let it shine, let it shine.

Heavenly Sunshine

Heav - en - ly sun - shine, heav - en - ly

sun - shine, Flood - ing my soul with glo - ry di - -

vine, _____ Heav - en - ly sun - shine, heav - en - ly

sun - shine, Hal - le - lu - jah, Je - sus is mine.

Where Is Heaven?

by Bliss Carman

Where is Heaven? Is it not
Just a friendly garden plot,
Walled with stone and roofed with sun,
Where the days pass one by one
Not too fast and not too slow,
Looking backward as they go
At the beauties left behind
To transport the pensive mind.

Does not Heaven begin that day
When the eager heart can say,
Surely God is in this place,
I have seen Him face to face
In the loveliness of flowers,
In the service of the showers,
And His voice has talked to me
In the sunlit apple tree.

God Make My Life a Little Light

by M. Bentham-Edwardsthat

God make my life a little light,
    Within the world to glow;
A tiny flame that burneth bright
    Wherever I may go.

God make my life a little flower,
    That giveth joy to all,
Content to bloom in native bower,
    Although its place be small.

God make my life a little staff,
    Whereon the weak may rest,
That so what health and strength I have
    May serve my neighbors best.

Jesus is Born

any years ago, in the town of Nazareth, a man named Joseph—a descendant of King David—and a woman named Mary planned to get married. A few weeks before the wedding was to take place, the Emperor Caesar Augustus sent out an important notice saying that a census would be taken. (A census is when all the people of a place are counted to find out how many there are.) "In order to do this," the order read, "all men must return to their place of birth." So Joseph and Mary packed their belongings and set off for Bethlehem, the place where Joseph had been born. It was a long ride, and Mary was very uncomfortable. You see, her belly was very, very big because she was going to have a baby—not Joseph's baby, but God's baby. Knowing his soon-to-be wife had a holy baby inside of her, Joseph took extra good care of her.

When they arrived in Bethlehem, the streets were noisier, dustier, and more crowded than Joseph remembered them to be. Men and women flooded the marketplace, vendors shouted out their wares, boys and girls played catch with stray pieces of fruit, dogs barked, cats meowed, and mice scurried under everybody's feet. Joseph was about to tell Mary that he recognized very few people when. . . .

"Joseph!" Mary moaned. "I just felt a pain in my belly. The baby is about to be born!" She winced and

waited for another pain to pass.

Quickly, Joseph led their donkey away from the crowds toward the outskirts of town. "We must find a place for you to be comfortable," he said, feeling nervous and excited at the same time. As they rode along, Mary clutched her belly, wincing with pain every few minutes. Soon they reached an old inn.

"Do you have any rooms?" he asked the innkeeper while Mary waited outside. "My wife is about to have a baby."

"Sorry," said the innkeeper, "but every room is full. Lots of people have come to Bethlehem because of the census."

Joseph returned to Mary, whose pains were coming every few seconds now, and they rode to another inn—but it too was full. So were the next three inns they tried. The last innkeeper took one look at Mary and suggested they go to the stables behind the inn. "At least it's quiet back there," he said kindly.

Just as they reached the stables, Mary let out a wail and minutes later gave birth to a tiny baby boy. "His name is Jesus," she said to Joseph. And they both wept with joy as they dressed God's Son in old cloths and placed him in a manger. (A manger is a trough filled with hay for animals to eat from.)

That evening, out in a pasture near Bethlehem, three shepherds watched their flocks. As the sky darkened around their cattle and

sheep, they suddenly saw a shimmery light, which got brighter and brighter until the entire pasture was lit up!

"That's the brightest star I've ever seen!" cried one of the shepherds, shielding his eyes.

"It's bigger than a star!" said another shepherd. "And it's getting bigger and brighter every second."

"Shhhh," said the third shepherd. "Do you hear that lovely music?"

The other shepherds nodded as they listened to a sweet melody that seemed to come from the brightness.

Suddenly, a beautiful angel appeared before them and they gasped with terror!

"Do not be afraid," the angel said in a soft, velvety voice. "I've come with joyful news. Today, in the town of Bethlehem, the Son of God has been born. He will be the King of the Jews. You must go and see for yourselves."

"W-where will we find him?" asked one of the shepherds. (The others were too filled with awe to speak, for they knew this angel had been sent by God.)

"Go to the inn at the farthest end of town," said the angel. "Behind it is a stable. You'll find the Baby Jesus in a manger." Then the angel disap-

peared and the sky was dark.

"Let's go to Bethlehem!" the three shepherds said at the same time. They gathered their flocks and headed into town under a starlit sky. A few hours later they reached the stable. Mary was busy feeding God's Son while Joseph watched with love in his eyes.

As the shepherds watched this beautiful scene, a warm, peaceful feeling came over them.

It was true! The shepherds now knew. The King of the Jews had been born! They spread the joyful news all over town, and crowds of people came to see God's Son for themselves. As they gazed at the tiny baby in the manger, their eyes filled with tears. They were very grateful that

God had blessed them with such a wonderful gift.

Meanwhile, on the same night Baby Jesus was born, three wise men in the east were looking up at the stars. These wise men had spent years studying astronomy, and they were very familiar with the night sky.

"I've never seen that one before," one of the wise men said with surprise as he pointed to an especially bright star.

"That star is a sign from God," another wise man said with excitement.

"God's letting us know that his Son, the King of the Jews, has been born!" said the third wise man.

With that, the three wise men packed up their few belongings,

including special gifts for the baby, and climbed on their camels. Then they set off for Jerusalem. You see, at that time Jerusalem was the most beautiful and popular city and they assumed they would find Baby Jesus there. As they rode through the hot, dry desert, the wise men grew more and more excited. They couldn't wait to worship their new King!

The three wise men traveled for many weeks. When they finally arrived in Jerusalem, they made an appointment with King Herod, Jerusalem's mean and jealous ruler,

for they thought he would know where they could find God's tiny Son.

"Your Majesty," said one of the wise men. "Where is the baby who has been born King of the Jews?"

King Herod looked confused, for he hadn't heard about Baby Jesus.

"We saw his star in the east and have come to worship him," another wise man explained.

"Worship him?" King Herod shouted angrily. "I'm the only king who should be worshiped!" Then he sent the wise men out and called together all his advisors and priests and teachers of the law. "Has anyone heard of

91

a baby boy that has been born to be King of the Jews?" he asked nervously.

"I have!" said one of his advisors. "The child lives with his parents in Bethlehem."

King Herod frowned. He ordered a servant to fetch the three wise men. "The baby boy you're searching for is in Bethlehem," he said when they once again stood before his throne. "Go there and find out the exact place he lives. Then come back and tell me all about him."

"But why do you want to know about him?" one of the wise men asked.

"So that I too may go and worship him," said King Herod. This, of course, was a lie. He really just wanted to learn more about this extraor-

dinary infant.

That evening, the three wise men climbed on their camels and headed toward Bethlehem. This time they knew exactly where they were going, for now they followed the bright star that had been in the sky on the night Baby Jesus was born. Brighter than anything else in the night sky, the star led them right to the quaint cottage where Joseph, Mary, and Baby Jesus were now living.

The wise men tied their camels to the outside gate, went to the front door, and knocked. Seconds later,

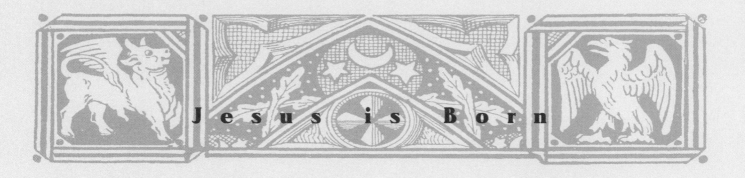

Jesus is Born

Mary invited them inside.

"We've come a long way," said one of the wise men, as he wiped his boots on the doormat.

"A bright star led us here," said another wise man, listening for the sounds of a baby.

"We'd like to worship our new King," said the third wise man.

"Follow me," Mary said, and she led them into a room where Joseph sat in front of a glowing fire. When they saw Baby Jesus, cooing and smiling in the cradle beside Joseph, the wise men sunk to their knees, overcome by a feeling of pure love and joy.

After several minutes of silence, the wise men, one by one, presented Baby Jesus with treasures.

"This is for you, great King," said one wise man, placing a bag of gold at the foot of the cradle. Then he moved away and the next wise man took his place.

"You will be the greatest of all men," the second wise man said to Baby Jesus. He placed a jar of myrrh next to the gold. (Myrrh is a special perfume that can only be worn by important men.) Then he moved away to make room for the last wise man.

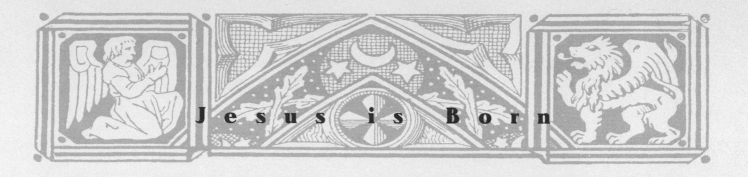

"This incense will make the air sweet," the third wise man explained to Mary and Joseph, placing a small jar between the gold and the myrrh. "Incense is pleasing to God. The tiny king in this cradle is both man and God."

Mary and Joseph thanked the wise men warmly. Then they all bowed their heads and prayed to God. They thanked him for bringing Baby Jesus—King of the Jews—into the world. Then the wise men left, feeling wonderfully blessed.

That night, the wise men slept at an inn where they all had the same strange dream. In the dream, a voice warned them not to return to King Herod. When the wise men woke up, they knew that the voice in the dream belonged to God. He had sent them a warning. So instead of traveling back to Jerusalem as they had planned, the three wise men went home along a different route.

King Herod eventually heard all about God's very special son—he was all anyone in the kingdom ever talked about. The story of Baby Jesus' birth was told over and over and over again. No one, including the three wise men, the three shepherds, Mary, or Joseph, would ever forget what happened on that miraculous night. Even today, all over the world, the birthday of Baby Jesus is still celebrated. But now it's known as Christmas.

Prayers

Now I lay me down to sleep,
I pray thee, Lord, thy child to keep:
Thy love be with me through the night
And wake me with the morning light.
Amen.

Lord, keep us safe this night,
Secure from all our fears.
May angels guard us while we sleep,
Till morning light appears.
Amen.